EMBRACING *THE SHADOW* WITHIN

A JOURNEY TO WHOLENESS

ASHA NYX

Copyright © 2024 by ASHA NYX

All rights are reserved, and no part of this publication may be reproduced, distributed, or transmitted in any manner, whether through photocopying, recording, or any other electronic or mechanical methods, without the explicit prior written permission of the publisher. This restriction applies to any form or means of reproduction or distribution.

Exceptions to this rule include brief quotations that may be incorporated into critical reviews, as well as certain other noncommercial uses that are allowed by copyright law. Any such usage must adhere to the specified conditions and permissions outlined by the copyright holder.

Formatted by HMDPUBLISHING

Contents

INTRODUCTION THE JOURNEY BEGINS 5

1. **MEETING OUR SHADOW** 12
   JOURNAL PROMPTS AND WORKSHEET: CHAPTER 1 17
   END-OF-CHAPTER EXERCISE 19
2. **THE FORMATION OF OUR SHADOW** 20
   JOURNAL PROMPTS AND WORKSHEET: CHAPTER 2 25
   END-OF-CHAPTER EXERCISE 27
3. **THE FIRST STEPS TO INTEGRATION** 29
   JOURNAL PROMPTS AND WORKSHEET: CHAPTER 3 34
   END-OF-CHAPTER EXERCISE 36
4. **TECHNIQUES FOR ADVANCED SHADOW WORK** 37
   JOURNAL PROMPTS AND WORKSHEET: CHAPTER 4 43
   END-OF-CHAPTER EXERCISE 45
5. **EMBRACING AND INTEGRATING THE SHADOW** 46
   JOURNAL PROMPTS AND WORKSHEET: CHAPTER 5 51
   END-OF-CHAPTER EXERCISE 53
6. **SUSTAINING THE SHADOW WORK PRACTICE** 54
   JOURNAL PROMPTS AND WORKSHEET: CHAPTER 6 59
   END-OF-CHAPTER EXERCISE 61
7. **TRANSFORMING THROUGH INTEGRATION** 62
   JOURNAL PROMPTS AND WORKSHEET: CHAPTER 7 67
   END-OF-CHAPTER EXERCISE 69
8. **LIVING IN WHOLENESS** 70
   THE ROLE OF SHADOW WORK IN WHOLENESS 71
   JOURNAL PROMPTS AND WORKSHEET: CHAPTER 8 75
   END-OF-CHAPTER EXERCISE 77

9. **STAYING CONNECTED TO YOUR SHADOW WORK JOURNEY** 78
   JOURNAL PROMPTS AND WORKSHEET: CHAPTER 9 83
   END-OF-CHAPTER EXERCISE 85

10. **THE COLLECTIVE SHADOW** 87
    UNDERSTANDING OUR SHARED HUMANITY 87
    JOURNAL PROMPTS AND WORKSHEET: CHAPTER 10 ... 93
    END-OF-CHAPTER EXERCISE 95

11. **THE POWER OF INTEGRATION IN EVERYDAY LIFE** 97
    PERSONAL REFLECTIONS: STORIES OF SHADOW WORK IN EVERYDAY LIFE 101
    JOURNAL PROMPTS AND WORKSHEET: CHAPTER 11...103
    END-OF-CHAPTER EXERCISE 105

12. **REFLECTING ON THE JOURNEY** 106
    EMBRACING YOUR WHOLE SELF 106
    JOURNAL PROMPTS AND WORKSHEET: CHAPTER 12 ... 111
    END-OF-CHAPTER EXERCISE 113

CONCLUSION 115
   A LIFE TRANSFORMED 115

INTRODUCTION
THE JOURNEY BEGINS

We all carry hidden parts within us—pieces of our psyche tucked away into the shadows. Some of these parts emerge as fleeting feelings of anger, jealousy, or inadequacy, while others linger quietly, influencing our decisions and behaviors in ways we barely notice. These hidden elements of ourselves make up what renowned psychologist Carl Jung called the "shadow." Shadow work is the courageous process of bringing these elements into the light, understanding their origins, and ultimately learning to embrace them as integral parts of who we are.

But what does it truly mean to embrace your shadow? And why is this journey so profoundly transformative? This book is your guide to uncovering and integrating the parts of yourself that you've kept hidden, whether intentionally or unknowingly. It is an invitation to embark on a journey of self-awareness, healing, and wholeness.

What is shadow work?

Shadow work is not a path for the faint-hearted, yet it is one that rewards those who dare to tread it with unparalleled self-discovery and peace. It involves turning toward the parts of yourself you may have long avoided—the anger you suppress, the fears you downplay, the jealousy you deny, and even the talents or desires you've abandoned out of fear of judgment.

Engaging with the shadow is not about "fixing" yourself or eradicating so-called flaws. It is about compassionately meeting these parts with curiosity and understanding. Think of shadow work as an excavation of your inner world. With each layer you uncover, you bring unconscious patterns and emotions to the surface, allowing them to be acknowledged and integrated.

For instance, imagine that you find yourself growing defensive every time a colleague questions your ideas. On the surface, it may seem like a minor annoyance, but shadow work invites you to ask deeper questions: Why do I react so strongly? What past experiences might have contributed to this feeling? What does this emotion want me to understand about myself?

By investigating these questions, you might discover that your defensiveness stems from a long-buried fear of inadequacy rooted in childhood. Shadow work doesn't stop at uncovering these wounds—it empowers you to heal them, transforming defensiveness into self-assurance and open communication.

THE ORIGINS AND IMPORTANCE OF SHADOW WORK

The concept of the shadow is deeply rooted in psychology, particularly in the work of Carl Jung. Jung believed that the shadow is the unconscious aspect of the self, formed by the traits, desires, and behaviors we reject or suppress. These rejected aspects are often labeled as "negative" or "unacceptable" based on societal, familial, or cultural expectations. Over time, the shadow grows, exerting influence on our lives in subtle but powerful ways.

While Jung provided the modern framework for understanding the shadow, the idea of confronting our hidden self is far older. Ancient myths and spiritual traditions have long depicted the journey of facing one's darkness. For example, in Greek mythology, the descent of Persephone into the underworld is a symbolic representation of exploring the shadow. Her eventual return to the surface signifies integration—embracing both the dark and light aspects of the self.

Shadow work is a timeless practice because it addresses a universal truth: every human being has unresolved wounds, repressed emotions, and hidden potential. In a world that often glorifies perfection and external success, shadow work offers a counterbalance, reminding us that true growth lies in self-acceptance and inner harmony.

Why This Book?

You may be wondering: Why should I choose this book as my companion on this journey? The truth is, shadow work can feel overwhelming. Many resources present it as an abstract, overly psychological process that leaves readers unsure of where to begin. This book is different. It is designed to make shadow work approachable, relatable, and practical.

Whether you are new to shadow work or have already dipped your toes into self-awareness practices, this book offers a roadmap tailored to your needs. Its goal is to demystify shadow work, breaking it down into manageable steps that empower you to engage with your inner world gently yet effectively.

Here's what sets this book apart:

- **Empathetic Guidance:** Throughout these pages, you will find a compassionate voice that understands the vulnerability of this journey. Shadow work is not about forcing yourself to face uncomfortable truths; it is about creating a safe, supportive environment to explore your inner world.
- **Balanced Approach:** This book weaves together insights from psychology, spirituality, and practical exercises. By combining these perspectives, it ensures a holistic understanding of the shadow that speaks to both your mind and soul.
- **Interactive Tools:** Shadow work isn't something you passively read about—it's a practice. This book includes journaling prompts, exercises, and guided meditations to help you actively engage with your shadow. It also provides real-life stories of individuals who have transformed their lives through this work, offering both inspiration and relatability.
- **Practical Applications:** Beyond self-awareness, shadow work has real-world benefits. This book will show you how

to apply shadow work to your relationships, career, creativity, and daily life. The goal is not just to understand yourself better but to live more authentically and joyfully.

THE BENEFITS OF SHADOW WORK

The rewards of shadow work extend far beyond emotional healing. By integrating your shadow, you unlock a deeper sense of wholeness and authenticity. Here are some of the profound benefits you can expect as you embark on this journey:

Improved Relationships: When you confront your shadow, you become less likely to project unresolved feelings onto others. This leads to healthier, more authentic relationships based on mutual understanding and respect.

Greater Emotional Resilience: Shadow work helps you navigate your emotions with grace and awareness. By understanding the roots of your triggers, you can respond to challenges with calmness rather than reactivity.

Enhanced Creativity and Potential: The shadow often contains hidden talents and desires that were suppressed out of fear or judgment. By embracing these aspects, you tap into a wellspring of creativity and motivation.

Inner Peace and Balance: Shadow work fosters a profound sense of self-acceptance. When you stop fighting against parts of yourself, you experience greater harmony and inner peace.

Authentic Living: Perhaps the greatest gift of shadow work is the ability to live authentically. By embracing your whole self—the light and the dark—you step into your full power and potential.

HOW TO USE THIS BOOK

This book is divided into four parts, each designed to guide you through a different stage of shadow work.

Here's what you can expect:

Part 1: Understanding the Shadow

Learn what the shadow is, how it forms, and why engaging with it is essential for personal growth. This section provides the foundation knowledge needed to embark on this journey.

Part 2: Engaging with Your Shadow

Explore practical techniques for connecting with your shadow, including journaling, meditation, and creative expression. These tools will help you uncover and engage with your hidden self.

Part 3: Healing and Integration

Discover how to transform your relationship with your shadow through self-compassion, forgiveness, and practical applications. This section focuses on bringing your shadow into harmony with your conscious self.

Part 4: The Journey Continues

Learn advanced shadow work techniques and how to sustain this practice over the long term. This section encourages you to embrace shadow work as an ongoing journey of growth and self-discovery.

At the end of each chapter, you will find journaling prompts and exercises to help you deepen your exploration. Take your time with these activities, and remember that shadow work is a process, not a race. Be patient with yourself and celebrate each step forward, no matter how small.

A GENTLE REMINDER

Before you dive into shadow work, it's important to acknowledge that this journey requires vulnerability and courage. There may be moments when you feel uncomfortable or unsure of how to proceed. That's okay. Shadow work isn't about achieving perfection or fixing you; it's about meeting yourself with love, curiosity, and acceptance.

As you move through this book, keep this reminder close to your heart: You are not broken. You are whole, even in your imperfections. The shadow is not your enemy; it is a part of you that longs to be seen, understood, and integrated. By embracing your shadow, you are stepping into the fullness of who you are—a brave, radiant, and authentic being.

Welcome to the journey of a lifetime. Let's begin.

Part 1

UNDERSTANDING THE SHADOW

Chapter 1
MEETING OUR SHADOW

We all have parts of ourselves that we hide—pieces tucked away into the corners of our minds, often without our conscious awareness. These aspects, collectively known as "the shadow," hold the traits, emotions, and desires we've suppressed or rejected over time. The shadow isn't inherently negative; rather, it's a reflection of the complexity of being human.

Meeting our shadow is the first step toward understanding it. In this chapter, we'll explore what the shadow is, how it formed, and how it shapes our lives. Through relatable stories, cultural references, and reflective practices, we'll begin the journey of uncovering and embracing the hidden aspects of ourselves.

UNDERSTANDING THE SHADOW

The shadow represents the parts of ourselves that we've been taught to hide. It develops as we grow, influenced by our upbringing, culture, and personal experiences. Traits that don't align with societal norms or family expectations—such as anger, vulnerability, ambition, or even joy—are pushed out of sight, creating the shadow.

For example:

A child who is scolded for being "too loud" may suppress their natural enthusiasm, leading to a quieter, more reserved demeanor in adulthood.

A person raised to "never cry" may bury their sadness, creating difficulty in processing emotions later in life.

These traits don't disappear; they retreat into the unconscious, subtly influencing how we think, feel, and behave. Shadow work involves bringing these hidden aspects into awareness, where they can be understood, accepted, and integrated.

WHY MEET OUR SHADOW?

Meeting our shadow isn't about fixing ourselves; it's about understanding the parts of us that have been left unexplored. The shadow holds not only suppressed emotions but also hidden potential, creativity, and wisdom. By engaging with our shadow, we gain:

- **Self-Awareness:** Understanding our shadow helps us recognize patterns and behaviors we've unconsciously adopted.
- **Emotional Freedom:** Releasing repressed emotions allows us to process them in healthy ways.
- **Authenticity:** By integrating our shadow, we can embrace our true selves, no longer held back by fear or shame.

THE SHADOW IN MYTH & CULTURE

Throughout history, myths and stories have served as mirrors for the human psyche, reflecting the struggles we face with our shadow. In many traditions, the hero's journey often involves confronting a dark, hidden force—a symbolic representation of the shadow.

Greek Mythology: Persephone's Descent

In Greek mythology, Persephone's descent into the underworld symbolizes the journey of facing our shadow. Initially taken against her will, she eventually embraces her role as queen of the underworld, finding strength and wisdom in the darkness. Her story reminds us that exploring the shadow can lead to transformation and empowerment.

JUNGIAN PSYCHOLOGY AND ARCHETYPES

Carl Jung, who popularized the concept of the shadow, believed it was a universal part of the human psyche. He connected the shadow to archetypes found in myths and culture, such as the Trickster, who embodies the repressed chaos we fear but also the creativity we need to thrive.

THE SHADOW IN LITERATURE & FILM

Literature and film often depict characters grappling with their shadow, offering relatable and accessible examples of this concept in action.

DR. JEKYLL AND MR. HYDE

Robert Louis Stevenson's The Strange Case of Dr. Jekyll and Mr. Hyde explores the duality of human nature. Dr. Jekyll's attempt to suppress his darker impulses results in the uncontrollable emergence of Mr. Hyde. This story illustrates how rejecting the shadow can lead to chaos, while integrating it can bring balance.

MODERN FILMS

Movies like Star Wars and Frozen also depict the shadow journey. Luke Skywalker's confrontation with Darth Vader represents his struggle to reconcile light and dark within himself. Similarly, Elsa's journey in Frozen mirrors the process of shadow work as she learns to accept her powers rather than fear them.

These stories resonate because they reflect a universal truth: embracing the shadow leads to wholeness and empowerment.

▲ **Personal Reflections:** Stories of Meeting the Shadow

Maria's Story: Facing Anger

Maria, a teacher in her 30s, prided herself on her calm demeanor. But one day, during a heated discussion with her spouse, she felt a wave of anger she couldn't control. "It was like a stranger had taken over me," she recalled.

Through shadow work, Maria realized her anger stemmed from years of suppressing her emotions to appear "perfect." As a child, she had been punished for showing frustration, so she buried it deep inside. By acknowledging this anger as part of her shadow, Maria learned to express her emotions constructively, improving her relationships and sense of self.

David's Story: Overcoming Jealousy

David, a software engineer, found himself becoming increasingly irritated when his partner pursued hobbies without him. At first, he dismissed his feelings as unimportant, but they continued to grow.

Shadow work revealed that David's jealousy stemmed from a fear of abandonment rooted in childhood experiences. Once he acknowledged this fear and began working through it, he could support his partner's independence while also creating opportunities to nurture their connection.

HOW THE SHADOW SHAPES OUR LIVES

The shadow's influence extends into every aspect of our lives, often without our awareness. By bringing the shadow into consciousness, we can begin to shift these patterns.

IN RELATIONSHIPS

- **Projection:** We may judge others for qualities we dislike in ourselves. For example, criticizing a friend's "selfishness" might reflect our own suppressed need for self-care.
- **Triggers:** Conflicts often arise when our shadow traits are mirrored in others, giving us an opportunity for growth.

IN CAREER

- **Fear of Failure:** Suppressed fear can lead to perfectionism or procrastination, hindering professional growth.
- **Imposter Syndrome:** Doubting our abilities may stem from unresolved feelings of inadequacy in our shadow.

STEPS TO MEETING OUR SHADOW

The process of meeting the shadow requires curiosity and compassion.

Here are some steps to begin:

NOTICE EMOTIONAL TRIGGERS

Pay attention to situations that evoke strong emotional reactions. These triggers often point to unresolved aspects of the shadow.

REFLECT ON JUDGMENTS

Notice the traits you criticize most in others. What might these judgments reveal about your own shadow?

EXPLORE THE SHADOW WITH CURIOSITY

Approach your shadow with an open mind. Ask, "What is this part of me trying to teach me?"

CREATE SPACE FOR REFLECTION

Dedicate time to practices like journaling, meditation, or visualization to connect with your shadow.

JOURNAL PROMPTS AND WORKSHEET: CHAPTER 1

REFLECTIVE JOURNAL PROMPTS

Use the prompts below to explore your relationship with your shadow. Take your time, writing freely and without judgment.

What qualities or traits do I most admire in others? How might these reflect parts of myself that I've suppressed?

_____
_____
_____
_____

What qualities or traits do I find most irritating in others? How might these reflect parts of my shadow?

_____
_____
_____
_____

Think of a recent emotional trigger. What happened, and how did I feel? What might this reaction reveal about my shadow?

_____
_____
_____
_____

What is one aspect of myself that I feel ashamed or uncomfortable about? Why do I feel this way?

_____
_____
_____
_____

Worksheet: Observing Emotional Triggers

Reflect on a recent emotional reaction and use the following questions to guide your exploration.

What situation triggered this reaction?

_____
_____
_____
_____

What emotions arose, and how did I respond?

_____
_____
_____
_____

Is there a pattern or recurring theme in these reactions?

_____
_____
_____
_____

What part of my shadow might be asking for attention?

_____
_____
_____
_____

END-OF-CHAPTER EXERCISE

Take a moment to sit quietly and reflect on what you've learned about your shadow in this chapter. Write a short letter to your shadow, expressing gratitude for what it has taught you.

Example Letter:

"Dear Shadow, Thank you for the lessons you've been trying to show me. I understand now that the parts of myself I've rejected hold wisdom and strength. I promise to meet you with compassion and curiosity as we continue this journey together."

Write your letter below:

_____
_____
_____
_____
_____
_____
_____
_____
_____
_____
_____
_____

Chapter 2
THE FORMATION OF OUR SHADOW

The shadow doesn't emerge fully formed; it develops over time, shaped by our early experiences, relationships, and societal conditioning. By understanding how the shadow is created, we can trace the origins of our unconscious traits and emotions, bringing clarity to the hidden forces that influence our lives.

In this chapter, we'll explore how childhood experiences, cultural expectations, and emotional wounds contribute to the shadow's formation. Through relatable examples, reflective questions, and practical exercises, we'll gain insight into the shadow's roots and begin to unravel its impact on our present-day behaviors.

THE EARLY FORMATION OF THE SHADOW

The shadow begins to take shape in childhood. During our early years, we are naturally expressive, curious, and unfiltered. We cry when we're hurt, laugh when we're happy, and explore the world with boundless energy. But as we grow, we start receiving messages from those around us—parents, teachers, and peers—about which behaviors are acceptable and which are not.

THE ROLE OF EARLY CONDITIONING

Children are highly attuned to the approval and disapproval of caregivers. When certain traits or emotions are met with rejection, punishment, or shame, we learn to suppress them. Over time, these suppressed aspects form the foundation of the shadow.

For example:

A child who is told, "Stop crying; it's not a big deal," may internalize the belief that expressing sadness is unacceptable. This child might grow into an adult who struggles to process grief or connect with their vulnerability.

A child who is labeled "too bossy" may suppress their natural leadership qualities, leading to difficulties asserting themselves later in life.

EMOTIONAL WOUNDS AND THE SHADOW

Beyond social conditioning, emotional wounds also play a significant role in shaping the shadow. Experiences of rejection, criticism, or trauma can leave lasting imprints, causing us to dissociate from parts of ourselves that feel unsafe or unworthy.

CULTURAL AND SOCIETAL INFLUENCES

Our shadow is not shaped solely by personal experiences; it is also influenced by the cultural and societal norms we are exposed to. These external forces dictate which traits, behaviors, and emotions are considered desirable or undesirable.

GENDER ROLES AND EXPECTATIONS

Gender norms are a significant factor in the formation of the shadow. From a young age, we are often taught behaviors that align with societal expectations of masculinity or femininity.

- **For Men:** Traditional masculinity often discourages vulnerability, emotional expression, and nurturing qualities. As a result, men may suppress these traits, leading to emotional disconnection or difficulty forming intimate relationships.
- **For Women:** Traditional femininity often prioritizes traits like nurturing, gentleness, and selflessness while discouraging assertiveness or ambition. Women may suppress these qualities, leading to challenges in advocating for themselves or pursuing personal goals.

CULTURAL NORMS AND BELIEFS

Cultural narratives about success, beauty, and morality also influence the shadow.

For example:

In cultures that value achievement, individuals may suppress traits like playfulness or rest, viewing them as unproductive.

In communities that stigmatize mental health struggles, individuals may bury emotions like anxiety or sadness, leading to unresolved pain.

THE SHADOW AND EMOTIONAL TRIGGERS

The shadow often reveals itself through emotional triggers—moments when we experience intense, seemingly disproportionate reactions to people or situations. These triggers act as mirrors, reflecting the parts of ourselves that remain unexamined.

UNDERSTANDING TRIGGERS

Triggers are not random; they are clues to the unresolved aspects of our shadow.

For example:

Feeling irritated by someone's confidence may reflect suppressed desires for self-expression.

Feeling jealous of a friend's success may point to an unmet longing for achievement or recognition.

⊥ **Personal Reflections:** Stories of Shadow Formation

Sophie's Story: The Fear of Being Seen

Sophie, a graphic designer, often felt anxious about sharing her work, despite positive feedback from clients. Through shadow work, she traced this fear back to childhood memories of being criticized for her creativity. "I remember showing my drawings to my teacher, and she told me to focus on more serious subjects," Sophie recalled.

This experience planted the belief that her creativity wasn't valuable, leading her to suppress her artistic confidence. By revisiting this memory and reframing her self-perception, Sophie began to embrace her creative gifts without fear.

Liam's Story: Suppressing Sadness

Liam, a firefighter, prided himself on being stoic and dependable. But when he found himself snapping at loved ones over small issues, he realized something deeper was at play. Shadow work revealed that Liam had suppressed feelings of sadness and vulnerability after losing a close friend.

"I was raised to believe that crying made you weak," Liam admitted. By acknowledging these suppressed emotions and allowing himself to grieve, Liam found greater emotional balance and improved his relationships.

UNCOVERING THE SHADOW'S PATTERNS

To better understand the shadow's influence, it's essential to identify recurring patterns in our thoughts, emotions, and behaviors. These patterns often reveal the underlying traits or wounds we've repressed.

COMMON SHADOW PATTERNS

- **Perfectionism:** Rooted in fears of inadequacy, perfectionism can lead to overworking or avoiding risks.
- **People-Pleasing:** Suppressing personal needs to gain approval can create resentment and burnout.
- **Avoidance:** Avoiding conflict or difficult emotions may stem from unresolved fears of rejection.

By identifying these patterns, we can begin to address the root causes and make conscious changes.

STEPS TO UNCOVER THE SHADOW

Reflect on Childhood Experiences

What traits or emotions were discouraged or criticized during your upbringing?

Are there specific memories that stand out as shaping your self-perception?

EXAMINE CULTURAL INFLUENCES

What societal norms have shaped your beliefs about success, worthiness, or identity?

How have these norms influenced the traits you suppress?

NOTICE EMOTIONAL TRIGGERS

Pay attention to situations that evoke strong emotional reactions.

Ask yourself, "What does this reaction reveal about my shadow?"

PRACTICE SELF-COMPASSION

Remember that the shadow is not your enemy; it is a part of you that longs to be understood.

JOURNAL PROMPTS AND WORKSHEET: CHAPTER 2

REFLECTIVE JOURNAL PROMPTS

Use the prompts below to explore the origins of your shadow. Write your responses in the space provided.

What traits or emotions were discouraged during your childhood? How have these experiences shaped your shadow?

_____
_____
_____
_____

What societal or cultural norms have influenced the traits you suppress?

_____
_____
_____
_____

Think of a recent emotional trigger. What happened, and how did you respond? What does this reveal about your shadow?

_____
_____
_____
_____

What recurring patterns do you notice in your relationships or behaviors? How might these patterns be connected to your shadow?

_____
_____
_____
_____

Worksheet: Tracing the Shadow's Roots

Use this worksheet to identify and reflect on the origins of your shadow.

_____
_____
_____
_____

What childhood experiences contributed to the formation of your shadow?

_____
_____
_____
_____

What emotions or traits have you suppressed, and why?

_____
_____
_____
_____

How have cultural or societal expectations influenced your shadow?

_____

_____

_____

_____

What part of your shadow is asking for attention now?

_____

_____

_____

_____

END-OF-CHAPTER EXERCISE

Take a moment to reflect on what you've learned about the formation of your shadow in this chapter. Write a letter to your younger self, offering them the validation and love they may not have received at the time.

Example Letter:

"Dear Younger Me,

I see the parts of you that were hidden away to feel safe or accepted. I want you to know that every part of you is valuable, and it's okay to feel, express, and embrace who you are. I promise to honor you and carry your courage as we continue to grow together."

Write your letter below:

Chapter 3
THE FIRST STEPS TO INTEGRATION

Understanding the shadow is only the beginning of the journey. Once we've met and acknowledged our shadow, the next step is to integrate it into our conscious awareness. Integration is not about erasing or "fixing" the shadow—it's about recognizing it as part of who we are and learning to work with it. This process involves compassion, curiosity, and a willingness to explore uncomfortable truths about ourselves.

In this chapter, we'll explore practical techniques for shadow integration, including reframing self-perception, working with emotional triggers, and using creative outlets for expression. Through real-life examples and reflective exercises, we'll learn how to take the first steps toward creating a more authentic and balanced self.

WHAT DOES INTEGRATION MEAN?

Integration is the process of bringing the shadow into the light of conscious awareness. It allows us to reclaim the traits and emotions we've suppressed, transforming them from sources of inner conflict into tools for growth and empowerment.

For example:

Suppressed anger, when acknowledged, can transform into assertiveness and boundary-setting.

Hidden vulnerability, when embraced, can become a source of deeper connection and empathy.

Integration doesn't mean acting out every impulse or shadow trait—it means finding healthy ways to express and honor these parts of ourselves.

WHY INTEGRATION IS ESSENTIAL

Without integration, the shadow can unconsciously shape our thoughts, emotions, and behaviors, often in ways that lead to self-sabotage or harm to our relationships. Integration brings these unconscious patterns into awareness, where we can address them constructively.

BENEFITS OF INTEGRATION

- **Emotional Resilience:** By facing and embracing our shadow, we develop greater emotional balance and flexibility.
- **Improved Relationships:** Integration helps us respond to others with empathy and authenticity, reducing projection and conflict.
- **Personal Empowerment:** Reclaiming suppressed traits unlocks hidden potential and creativity.

PRACTICAL TECHNIQUES FOR INTEGRATION

The journey of integration requires ongoing effort and practice. Here are some foundational techniques to begin integrating your shadow:

1. REFRAME YOUR SELF-PERCEPTION

Integration begins with seeing the shadow as a source of strength rather than weakness. Instead of labeling shadow traits as "bad" or "undesirable," recognize their hidden value.

Example:

- **Reframing Anger:** Instead of viewing anger as harmful, see it as a signal that your boundaries have been crossed. By honoring this message, you can learn to assert yourself constructively.

- **Reframing Vulnerability:** Vulnerability may feel uncomfortable, but it is also the foundation for authentic connection and intimacy.
- **Practice:** Write down one shadow trait you've suppressed and list three positive qualities it could represent.

2. **WORK WITH EMOTIONAL TRIGGERS.**

Emotional triggers are powerful opportunities for integration. When we experience a strong reaction, it's often because our shadow is being activated.

Steps to Work with Triggers:

- **Pause and Reflect:** When triggered, take a moment to pause and observe your reaction without judgment.
- **Ask Questions:** Reflect on the situation. "What am I feeling? What does this remind me of? What part of my shadow might be involved?"
- **Respond, Not React:** Instead of reacting impulsively, choose a conscious response that aligns with your values.

Example:

If a colleague's assertiveness triggers irritation, consider whether their behavior reflects a trait you've suppressed. Could it be that you've buried your own assertiveness, leading to discomfort when you see it in others?

3. **EXPRESS THE SHADOW THROUGH CREATIVITY**

Creative outlets provide a safe and constructive way to explore and express the shadow. Art, music, writing, and movement can help externalize hidden emotions and traits, making them easier to understand and integrate.

Ideas for Creative Expression:

- **Art:** Paint or draw an image representing your shadow. Focus on colors, shapes, and textures that capture its energy.

- **Writing:** Create a fictional story or poem where your shadow is a character. Explore its desires, fears, and motivations.
- **Movement:** Use dance or physical movement to embody your shadow traits. For example, move with strength to express suppressed anger or fluidity to connect with buried vulnerability.

Example:

A writer struggling with self-doubt might create a character embodying their shadow. By writing the character's story, they can gain new insights into their own fears and desires.

- **Personal Reflections:** Stories of Integration

Ana's Story: Reclaiming Creativity

Ana, a marketing professional, felt disconnected from her creativity after years of focusing on practical goals. Through shadow work, she realized that her artistic side had been suppressed due to childhood messages that creativity wasn't "serious" or "useful."

By engaging in creative practices like painting and journaling, Ana began to reconnect with her creative self. This not only enriched her personal life but also brought fresh ideas and innovation to her career.

Ryan's Story: Embracing assertiveness

Ryan, a customer service manager, struggled with people-pleasing, often saying "yes" to requests even when it caused stress. Shadow work revealed that Ryan had suppressed his assertiveness after being labeled "difficult" as a child.

By reframing assertiveness as a positive quality, Ryan started practicing boundary-setting in small, manageable ways. Over time, he found that honoring his own needs improved both his relationships and his self-esteem.

OVERCOMING RESISTANCE TO INTEGRATION

Resistance is a natural part of shadow work. It's common to feel discomfort, fear, or self-judgment when confronting suppressed traits. Recognizing and addressing this resistance is a crucial step in the process.

Common Forms of Resistance:

- **Denial:** "That's not part of me."
- **Avoidance:** "I don't want to think about this right now."
- **Self-Criticism:** "I shouldn't feel this way."

How to Overcome Resistance:

- **Practice compassion:** remind yourself that the shadow is a natural and universal part of being human.
- **Start Small:** Focus on manageable aspects of the shadow rather than tackling everything at once.
- **Seek Support:** Share your journey with a trusted friend, therapist, or shadow work group.

JOURNAL PROMPTS AND WORKSHEET: CHAPTER 3

REFLECTIVE JOURNAL PROMPTS

What shadow traits have I recently become aware of? How might these traits serve a positive purpose in my life?

_____

_____

_____

_____

Think of a recent emotional trigger. What happened, and how did I respond? How might this reaction be connected to my shadow?

_____

_____

_____

_____

What creative outlets could I use to explore and express my shadow? How might these practices help me integrate it?

_____

_____

_____

_____

What resistance do I feel when engaging with my shadow? How can I approach this resistance with curiosity and compassion?

_____
_____
_____
_____

Worksheet: Transforming Shadow Traits

Use this worksheet to explore and reframe a shadow trait.

What shadow trait am I focusing on?

_____
_____
_____
_____

What situations or emotions bring this trait to the surface?

_____
_____
_____
_____

What positive qualities or strengths might this trait represent?

_____
_____
_____
_____

How can I express or honor this trait in a healthy way?

_____
_____
_____
_____

END-OF-CHAPTER EXERCISE

Take a moment to reflect on your journey of integration so far. Write a letter to your shadow, expressing your commitment to working with it constructively.

Example Letter:

"Dear Shadow,

Thank you for revealing yourself to me. I see now that the parts of myself I've suppressed hold incredible value and strength. I promise to approach you with patience and compassion, learning from the lessons you offer. Together, we can create a more authentic and empowered version of who I am."

Write your letter below:

_____
_____
_____
_____
_____
_____
_____
_____
_____

Chapter 4
TECHNIQUES FOR ADVANCED SHADOW WORK

Once you've begun integrating your shadow and understanding its origins, the journey doesn't stop there. Advanced shadow work dives deeper, uncovering hidden layers of the unconscious and addressing complex emotions, patterns, and beliefs. This chapter introduces advanced techniques to further connect with your shadow, including inner child healing, ancestral work, dream exploration, and collective shadow analysis.

By engaging with these practices, you'll expand your self-awareness and continue your journey toward authenticity and balance.

Inner Child Healing: Revisiting the Past

The inner child represents the part of us that retains the emotions, memories, and beliefs formed during childhood. Many aspects of the shadow stem from childhood experiences, making inner child work an essential component of advanced shadow work.

CONNECTING WITH THE INNER CHILD

The inner child often carries wounds from unmet needs, rejection, or criticism. These wounds manifest as insecurities or fears in adulthood.

By revisiting and nurturing the inner child, we can heal these wounds and release the patterns they create.

Steps to Inner Child Healing:

Visualization Exercise:

Sit in a quiet space and imagine your younger self. What age comes to mind? Observe their emotions, body language, and surroundings.

Approach your inner child with kindness and ask, "What do you need from me?" Offer them love, reassurance, and validation.

Writing Letters:

Write a letter to your younger self, acknowledging their struggles and offering words of comfort. Then, write a letter from your inner child to your adult self, allowing them to express their feelings freely.

Example:

As an adult, Alex struggled with perfectionism. Inner child work revealed that Alex's need to "get everything right" stemmed from a childhood fear of disappointing their parents. By comforting and affirming their inner child, Alex began to let go of this fear and embrace imperfection.

Ancestral Shadow Work: Healing Generational Patterns

The shadow is not only personal—it is also shaped by ancestral influences. Traumas, beliefs, and behaviors can be passed down through generations, creating patterns that impact us unconsciously.

IDENTIFYING ANCESTRAL SHADOWS

Recurring family dynamics, such as cycles of addiction, fear of scarcity, or unresolved grief, may point to ancestral shadows.

Reflect on your family history: What patterns, values, or unspoken rules have shaped your upbringing?

Techniques for Ancestral Healing:

Family Tree Exploration:

Create a family tree and note significant events, patterns, or traumas in your lineage. Reflect on how these experiences might have influenced your beliefs or behaviors.

Ancestral Rituals:

Light a candle or place an object that symbolizes your ancestors in a quiet space. Offer gratitude for their contributions and set an intention to release any burdens or patterns that no longer serve you.

Meditative Connection:

During meditation, visualize a line of ancestors standing behind you. Imagine them passing wisdom or healing energy to you. Thank them for their guidance and support.

Dream Exploration: Messages from the Unconscious

Dreams provide a direct line to the unconscious mind, offering symbolic insights into the shadow. Advanced shadow work often involves analyzing and engaging with dreams to uncover hidden emotions, desires, and truths.

INTERPRETING DREAMS

Dreams communicate through metaphor and symbolism.

For example:

A dream of falling might reflect fears of failure or loss of control.

Encountering a shadowy figure might symbolize a repressed part of yourself seeking acknowledgment.

Steps to Explore Dreams:

Keep a Dream Journal:

Write down your dreams as soon as you wake up, noting symbols, emotions, and key events.

Reflect on Key Symbols:

Ask, "What does this symbol represent to me personally? How might it connect to my shadow?"

Active Imagination:

Revisit the dream in your mind and imagine interacting with its elements. Ask the shadowy figure, "What message do you have for me?"

Example:

Lily dreamt of being chased by a faceless figure. Shadow work revealed that the figure represented her suppressed fear of failure. By acknowledging this fear, Lily began to take calculated risks and pursue her goals.

EXPLORING THE COLLECTIVE SHADOW

The collective shadow represents the unconscious beliefs, biases, and behaviors of society. Engaging with the collective shadow can deepen your understanding of cultural and systemic influences on your personal shadow.

RECOGNIZING THE COLLECTIVE SHADOW

The collective shadow often manifests in societal norms, stereotypes, or systemic injustices.

Reflect on how societal messages about gender, race, success, or morality have shaped your beliefs or suppressed traits.

Steps to Work with the Collective Shadow:

Self-Education:

Learn about systemic issues and cultural narratives that influence your identity and beliefs.

Engage in community reflection:

Join groups or discussions focused on exploring collective shadows, such as workshops on bias, privilege, or cultural healing.

Take conscious action:

Use your awareness of the collective shadow to make informed, compassionate choices in your community and relationships.

Personal Reflections: Stories of Advanced Shadow Work

Elena's Story: Ancestral Healing

Elena often felt an inexplicable fear of financial instability, despite having a stable career. Shadow work revealed that this fear was rooted in her grandmother's experiences of poverty during the war. By engaging in ancestral rituals and reframing her beliefs, Elena began to trust in her ability to create abundance.

James's Story: Insights Through Dreams

James had recurring dreams of being trapped in a small room. Through shadow work, he discovered that the room symbolized his feelings of being "boxed in" by societal expectations. By addressing these feelings, James found the courage to pursue a career aligned with his passions.

STEPS FOR ADVANCED INTEGRATION

Advanced shadow work requires commitment, patience, and self-compassion. Here are some steps to guide your practice:

Deepen Self-Reflection:

Use tools like journaling, meditation, or therapy to explore hidden layers of your shadow.

Engage in dialogue:

Whether through dream exploration or inner child work, open a conversation with the parts of yourself that feel neglected or misunderstood.

Practice Gratitude:

Acknowledge the wisdom and strength your shadow offers. Thank it for its role in your growth.

Seek Support:

Work with a therapist, coach, or shadow work group to navigate complex emotions and patterns.

JOURNAL PROMPTS AND WORKSHEET: CHAPTER 4

REFLECTIVE JOURNAL PROMPTS

What emotions, traits, or patterns in my life feel connected to childhood experiences? How can I begin to heal these connections?

_____

_____

_____

_____

What recurring family patterns have I noticed? How might these patterns influence my beliefs or behaviors?

_____

_____

_____

_____

Think of a recent dream that felt significant. What symbols or emotions stood out? What might they reveal about my shadow?

_____

_____

_____

_____

How have societal messages shaped my perception of myself? What parts of my identity have I suppressed because of these messages?

_____
_____
_____
_____

Worksheet: Exploring Advanced Shadow Layers

Use this worksheet to reflect on different dimensions of your shadow:

Inner Child: What memory or experience from childhood feels unresolved? How can I offer comfort or healing to my younger self?

_____
_____
_____
_____

Ancestral Patterns: What family story, belief, or pattern feels most relevant to my shadow?

_____
_____
_____
_____

Dream Symbolism: What is one symbol from a recent dream that stands out? What does it represent to me?

_____
_____
_____
_____

Collective Shadow: How have cultural norms or biases influenced my shadow? How can I challenge or reframe these influences?

_____
_____
_____
_____

END-OF-CHAPTER EXERCISE

Write a letter to your shadow, reflecting on what you've uncovered in this chapter. Offer gratitude for the deeper layers it has revealed and set an intention for continued growth.

Example Letter:

"Dear Shadow,

Thank you for guiding me through the deeper layers of who I am. I see now that my past, my family, and my dreams all hold pieces of you, waiting to be understood. I promise to approach these layers with curiosity, courage, and compassion as I continue this journey."

Write your letter below:

_____
_____
_____
_____
_____
_____
_____
_____

Chapter 5
EMBRACING AND INTEGRATING THE SHADOW

Shadow work reaches its most transformative stage when we actively embrace and integrate the shadow into our daily lives. Integration is about creating harmony between the conscious and unconscious parts of ourselves, allowing us to live authentically and without fear of our hidden traits. This chapter explores practical methods for integrating the shadow into our relationships, decision-making, and sense of self.

Through stories, exercises, and reflective practices, we will learn how to welcome our shadow as a valuable part of who we are and harness its wisdom to enrich our lives.

WHY EMBRACE THE SHADOW?

Many of us have spent years, even decades, running from our shadow. Embracing it might feel counterintuitive, especially if we associate shadow traits with shame or fear. But the truth is that the shadow holds untapped potential, creativity, and resilience.

BY EMBRACING OUR SHADOW:

We Become Whole: No longer divided between our conscious and unconscious selves, we gain a sense of inner harmony.

We Build Authentic Relationships: Understanding our shadow helps us reduce projection, improve empathy, and foster deeper connections with others.

We Unlock Hidden Strengths: Traits once buried in the shadow—such as assertiveness, vulnerability, or playfulness—become sources of empowerment when reintegrated.

Practices for embracing the shadow

1. **Mirror Work**: Seeing Your Shadow Clearly

Mirror work involves looking directly at yourself—literally and metaphorically. By facing your reflection and speaking affirmations, you create a safe space to connect with your shadow.

How to Practice Mirror Work:

Stand in front of a mirror and maintain eye contact with yourself.

Repeat affirmations such as:

"I accept every part of myself, even the parts I don't fully understand."

"I am willing to see the truth of who I am."

If uncomfortable emotions arise, acknowledge them without judgment.

Example:

Jenna struggled with self-criticism, often feeling unworthy. Through mirror work, she began to notice the harsh judgments she directed at herself and practiced replacing them with affirmations of self-acceptance. Over time, this softened her inner dialogue and allowed her to connect with her shadow compassionately.

2. **Practicing vulnerability:** Vulnerability is a gateway to shadow integration. By allowing ourselves to be seen—flaws and all—we create opportunities for authentic connection and healing.

Share an honest thought or feeling with someone you trust. For example, "I've been feeling insecure about this project, and I'm trying to understand why."

Acknowledge discomfort as it arises, reminding yourself that vulnerability is a strength, not a weakness.

Example:

Marco avoided talking about his emotions, fearing it would make him seem weak. Through shadow work, he practiced opening up to his partner about his feelings. This not only deepened their relationship but also helped Marco embrace his emotional side as a source of strength.

3. **Creative Integration:** Creative expression provides a non-linear, intuitive way to engage with the shadow. Whether through writing, art, or movement, creativity allows us to externalize and explore suppressed traits.

Ideas for Creative Integration:

- **Art:** Create a painting or drawing that represents your shadow.
- **Journaling:** Write a letter to a specific shadow trait, asking it what it needs from you.
- **Dance or Movement:** Use movement to embody shadow traits like anger, sadness, or joy.

Example:

Kara, a musician, realized she had suppressed her playful side to meet professional expectations. Through improvised singing and dancing, she reconnected with her inner child, infusing her music with renewed passion.

INTEGRATING THE SHADOW IN RELATIONSHIPS

Our relationships often act as mirrors for the shadow, reflecting back the traits and emotions we've disowned. By bringing awareness to these dynamics, we can create more authentic and compassionate connections.

1. **Recognizing Projection:** projection occurs when we attribute suppressed traits or feelings to others. For example, if we judge someone as "selfish," it may reflect our own suppressed desire to prioritize our needs.

Steps to Address Projection:

Notice when a strong emotional reaction arises in a relationship.

Ask yourself, "What does this reaction reveal about my own shadow?"

Reflect on how reclaiming this trait might bring balance to your life.

2. **Setting Boundaries with Compassion**

Integration often requires recalibrating our boundaries. By recognizing and honoring our needs, we show respect for both ourselves and others.

Example:

If you've suppressed assertiveness, practice setting small, clear boundaries. For instance, saying, "I need time to think before I make a decision," can help you honor your limits without conflict.

▲ **Personal Reflections:** Stories of Integration

Naomi's Story: Balancing Independence

Naomi, a business owner, prided herself on being independent but often felt isolated. Through shadow work, she realized she had suppressed her need for connection, viewing it as a weakness. By embracing this need and seeking support from friends and colleagues, Naomi found greater balance and fulfillment in her life.

Derek's Story: Reclaiming Confidence

Derek, an artist, frequently downplayed his achievements, fearing he would seem arrogant. Shadow work revealed that his humility masked a suppressed desire to celebrate his accomplishments. By reclaiming this confidence, Derek began sharing his work more openly, attracting new opportunities and recognition.

CHALLENGES IN INTEGRATION

Integration is a process, and it's natural to encounter challenges along the way. Here are some common obstacles and strategies for overcoming them:

1. **Fear of judgment:** You may worry about how others will react to your integrated self.

    Solution: Remind yourself that shadow work is for your growth, not others' approval. Those who value authenticity will support your journey.

2. **Imposter Syndrome:** You might feel like you're "pretending" when reclaiming shadow traits.

    Solution: recognize that growth is a process. It's okay to feel uncomfortable as you integrate new aspects of yourself.

3. **Relapse into Old Patterns:** It's common to fall back into familiar habits during stressful times.

    Solution: Approach relapses with compassion. Use them as opportunities to deepen your understanding of your shadow.

JOURNAL PROMPTS AND WORKSHEET: CHAPTER 5

REFLECTIVE JOURNAL PROMPTS

What shadow traits have I begun to embrace? How have they enriched my life?

_____

_____

_____

_____

Think of a recent conflict or trigger in a relationship. What did it reveal about my shadow?

_____

_____

_____

_____

What creative outlet could I use to express a shadow trait? How might this practice support my integration journey?

_____

_____

_____

_____

What fears or resistance do I feel about fully integrating my shadow? How can I approach these feelings with compassion?

___

Worksheet: Embracing Shadow Traits

Use this worksheet to explore a nd embrace a shadow trait.

What shadow trait am I focusing on?

___

What positive qualities might this trait represent?

___

How can I express this trait in a healthy, constructive way?

___

What relationships or situations can help me practice integrating this trait?

_____
_____
_____
_____

END-OF-CHAPTER EXERCISE

Write a letter to yourself, reflecting on the progress you've made in integrating your shadow. Celebrate the courage it takes to embrace your full self.

Example Letter:

"Dear Self,

I'm proud of the steps I've taken to embrace every part of who I am. The journey hasn't always been easy, but I see the strength and wisdom I've gained through this process. I promise to continue approaching myself with love and compassion, knowing that integration is a lifelong practice."

Write your letter below:

_____
_____
_____
_____
_____
_____
_____
_____

Chapter 6
SUSTAINING THE SHADOW WORK PRACTICE

Shadow work is not a one-time process—it is a lifelong journey of growth, self-awareness, and integration. Once you've begun exploring and embracing your shadow, the challenge becomes maintaining this practice in the midst of life's complexities. Shadow work requires commitment, adaptability, and a willingness to revisit the process as new experiences arise.

This chapter focuses on strategies for sustaining shadow work as part of your ongoing personal development. You'll learn how to navigate setbacks, deepen your practice over time, and integrate shadow work into your daily routines.

THE IMPORTANCE OF CONSISTENCY IN SHADOW WORK

Shadow work often reveals layers of insights over time. As we encounter new challenges, relationships, and phases of life, previously unexamined aspects of our shadow come to light. A consistent practice ensures that we remain aware of these changes and continue to grow.

Why consistency matters

- **Builds Emotional Resilience**: Regular shadow work helps you respond to triggers and challenges with greater awareness and balance.

- **Deepens Self-Understanding**: Each layer of the shadow reveals new insights, expanding your understanding of yourself.
- **Supports Authentic Living**: By staying connected to your shadow, you can make choices aligned with your true self.

BUILDING A SHADOW WORK ROUTINE

Creating a sustainable routine ensures that shadow work becomes a natural and manageable part of your life.

KEY COMPONENTS OF A SHADOW WORK ROUTINE

- **Daily Reflection:** Spend a few minutes each day reflecting on emotional triggers, patterns, or judgments. Journaling can be a helpful tool for this practice.
- **Regular Check-Ins:** Dedicate time each week or month to review your shadow work journey. What new insights have emerged? What challenges are you facing?
- **Mindfulness Practices**: Use mindfulness techniques, such as meditation or deep breathing, to stay present with your emotions and reactions.
- **Creative Expression:** Incorporate art, writing, or movement into your routine to explore and express your shadow.

NAVIGATING SETBACKS AND RESISTANCE

Setbacks are a natural part of any growth process. Whether it's a challenging situation that reactivates old patterns or a period of avoidance, it's important to approach setbacks with compassion and curiosity.

Common challenges in sustaining shadow work

- **Avoidance:** You might feel tempted to ignore or dismiss your shadow when it brings up discomfort.
- **Overwhelm:** Deep emotions or complex patterns can feel difficult to process.

- **Relapse into Old Habits**: Stress or external pressures might lead you to revert to familiar behaviors.

STRATEGIES TO OVERCOME CHALLENGES

- **Practice Self-Compassion:** Remind yourself that setbacks are part of the process. Growth is not linear.
- **Break It Down:** If shadow work feels overwhelming, focus on small, manageable steps, such as exploring a single emotion or trigger.
- **Seek Support:** Reach out to a trusted friend, therapist, or support group to help you navigate challenging moments.

DEEPENING YOUR SHADOW WORK PRACTICE

Once you've established a routine, you may wish to deepen your shadow work by exploring new techniques and dimensions of your unconscious.

Advanced Techniques for Sustained Growth

- **Dream Work:** Pay attention to recurring dreams and symbols. Use journaling or active imagination to explore their meaning.
- **Body Awareness:** Notice where emotions or shadow traits manifest in your body. Practices like yoga or somatic therapy can help release stored tension.
- **Inner Dialogue:** Engage in a written or spoken dialogue with your shadow, asking it questions and listening to its responses.

INCORPORATING SHADOW WORK INTO DAILY LIFE

- **Mindful observation:** Notice how your shadow influences your thoughts, actions, and relationships throughout the day.
- **Conscious Communication:** Use shadow work insights to improve how you express your needs and respond to others.

- **Embracing Opportunities for Growth:** Treat conflicts and challenges as opportunities to learn more about your shadow.

Personal reflections: stories of sustained shadow work

Sophia's Story: Learning from Relapses

Despite her shadow work practice, Sophia, a social worker, fell into old patterns of overcommitting to others. "At first, I felt like I'd failed," she shared. "But then I realized that this relapse was an opportunity to deepen my self-awareness." By revisiting her need for external validation, Sophia uncovered new layers of her shadow and reaffirmed her boundaries.

Jason's Story: Integrating Shadow Work into Daily Life

Jason, a father of two, used shadow work to address his frustration during parenting challenges. By reflecting on his triggers, he realized they stemmed from his own childhood experiences of feeling unheard. "Whenever I feel myself reacting, I take a breath and ask, 'What is this really about?'" This practice helped Jason respond to his children with greater patience and empathy.

Celebrating Progress

Shadow work is a lifelong journey, and it's important to recognize and celebrate the progress you've made along the way.

Signs of Growth

You notice emotional triggers more quickly and respond with awareness.

You feel more comfortable expressing vulnerability and setting boundaries.

You experience a deeper sense of connection and authenticity in your relationships.

WAYS TO CELEBRATE YOUR JOURNEY

- **Reflect on Milestones:** Look back on the insights and transformations you've achieved.

- **Create a Ritual:** Light a candle or write a gratitude list to honor your progress.
- **Share Your Story:** Talk about your shadow work journey with someone you trust or in a supportive community.

JOURNAL PROMPTS AND WORKSHEET: CHAPTER 6

Reflective Journal Prompts

What challenges or setbacks have I faced in my shadow work journey? What lessons have these moments taught me?

_____

_____

_____

_____

What practices have helped me sustain my shadow work? How can I make them a regular part of my life?

_____

_____

_____

_____

Think of a recent situation where I felt triggered. How did I respond, and what does this reveal about my shadow?

_____

_____

_____

_____

What aspects of my shadow have I embraced over time? How have they enriched my life?

_____

_____

_____
_____

Worksheet: Sustaining Shadow Work

Use this worksheet to create a personalized plan for maintaining your shadow work practice.

_____
_____
_____

What practices will I include in my shadow work routine?

_____
_____
_____

How often will I dedicate time to shadow work?

_____
_____
_____

What challenges do I anticipate, and how will I address them?

_____
_____
_____

Who can I turn to for support when I need it?

_____
_____
_____
_____

END-OF-CHAPTER EXERCISE

Write a letter to your future self, reflecting on your commitment to sustaining your shadow work practice. Offer encouragement and remind yourself of the progress you've made.

Example Letter:

"Dear Future Me,

I know that shadow work is not always easy, but I trust in your ability to keep growing and learning. Remember that every step forward, no matter how small, is a victory. Celebrate your progress and continue approaching yourself with compassion and curiosity. I believe in your strength and resilience."

Write your letter below:

_____
_____
_____
_____
_____
_____
_____
_____
_____

Chapter 7
TRANSFORMING THROUGH INTEGRATION

Integration is not just about acknowledging the shadow but actively using its lessons to transform your life. Transformation occurs when the previously hidden parts of us are no longer a source of conflict but a foundation for growth. By embracing the shadow and weaving its wisdom into our choices, relationships, and creativity, we become more whole and authentic.

This chapter explores how shadow integration can lead to profound personal transformation. Through practical strategies and real-life examples, you'll learn how to harness the power of your shadow to enhance your relationships, embrace your purpose, and unlock your potential.

THE NATURE OF TRANSFORMATION

Transformation through shadow work is not a single moment of change but a continuous unfolding. As we integrate more of ourselves, we become freer to live with intention and authenticity.

WHAT TRANSFORMATION LOOKS LIKE

- **Freedom from Fear:** Shadow work reduces the unconscious fears that hold us back, empowering us to take bold steps toward our goals.

- **Strengthened Relationships:** By owning our shadow, we reduce projection and connect with others from a place of empathy and understanding.
- **Aligned Living**: Integration helps us align our choices with our values and passions, creating a more fulfilling life.

HOW INTEGRATION FUELS TRANSFORMATION

The shadow holds not only our fears and insecurities but also our strengths, creativity, and potential. When we integrate these aspects, we unlock new possibilities for growth and fulfillment.

1. RECLAIMING SUPPRESSED STRENGTHS

Many shadow traits are hidden strengths waiting to be rediscovered. For example:

- **Suppressed Assertiveness:** When integrated, this becomes confidence in setting boundaries and advocating for yourself.
- **Hidden Playfulness:** Embracing this can lead to greater joy, creativity, and resilience.

Example:

Rita, a lawyer, realized she had suppressed her playful side due to societal expectations of professionalism. Through shadow work, she began incorporating humor and creativity into her work, which improved her relationships with colleagues and clients.

2. TRANSFORMING LIMITING BELIEFS

The shadow often contains limiting beliefs we've internalized over time. By addressing and reframing these beliefs, we open ourselves to new possibilities.

Steps to Transform Limiting Beliefs:

- **Identify the Belief:** Write down a belief that feels restrictive (e.g., "I'm not creative").

- **Explore Its Origins:** Reflect on where this belief might have come from. Was it a message you received as a child or from society?
- **Reframe the belief:** Replace it with an empowering statement (e.g., "Creativity is a skill I can nurture and grow").

3. **USING THE SHADOW AS A CREATIVE FORCE**

The shadow is a wellspring of creativity. By engaging with it, we can unlock new ideas, perspectives, and solutions.

CREATIVE PRACTICES FOR TRANSFORMATION:

Journaling: Use free writing to explore shadow themes and uncover new insights.

Storytelling: Write a fictional story where your shadow traits are characters. How do they interact and resolve conflict?

Artistic Expression: Create art that represents your transformation through shadow work.

TRANSFORMATION IN RELATIONSHIPS

Integration doesn't just benefit us—it also transforms our relationships by fostering authenticity, empathy, and mutual growth.

1. **AUTHENTIC CONNECTION**

When we integrate our shadow, we can show up in relationships as our whole selves, free from the masks we once wore.

Example:

Dylan struggled with vulnerability in his marriage, often hiding his emotions to appear strong. Through shadow work, he realized this pattern stemmed from a fear of rejection. By embracing his vulnerability, Dylan built deeper intimacy and trust with his partner.

2. REDUCING CONFLICT

Projection often causes conflict in relationships. When we own our shadow, we can approach disagreements with greater understanding and compassion.

Example: Lisa often felt irritated by her friend's confidence, which she perceived as arrogance. Shadow work revealed that Lisa had suppressed her own confidence due to fear of being judged. By reclaiming this trait, she not only resolved her resentment but also strengthened her friendship.

EMBRACING PURPOSE THROUGH SHADOW WORK

Shadow work can help clarify your values and purpose by uncovering hidden desires and strengths. By integrating these insights, we can align our actions with what truly matters to us.

- **Reflect on Suppressed Passions:** What interests or dreams have you set aside due to fear or judgment?
- **Connect to Your Values:** What qualities or causes feel most meaningful to you?
- **Take Small Steps:** Use what you've learned through shadow work to take intentional actions toward your goals.

Example:

Through shadow work, Maya uncovered her long-buried desire to write. At first, she hesitated, fearing her work wouldn't be "good enough." By embracing her shadow, Maya started writing regularly, eventually publishing a book that aligned with her purpose of inspiring others.

PERSONAL REFLECTIONS: STORIES OF TRANSFORMATION

Omar's Story: Rediscovering Leadership

Omar, a manager, avoided taking risks at work, fearing failure. Shadow work revealed that this fear stemmed from childhood experiences of being criticized for mistakes. By reframing failure as an opportunity for growth, Omar began leading with confidence and creativity, inspiring his team and achieving greater success.

Elena's Story: Embracing emotional depth

Elena often suppressed her sadness, believing it made her weak. Shadow work helped her see sadness as a natural and necessary emotion. By embracing her emotional depth, Elena strengthened her relationships and discovered a talent for helping others, process their own feelings.

SIGNS OF TRANSFORMATION THROUGH INTEGRATION

How do you know if your shadow work is transforming your life? Here are some common signs:

- **Emotional Awareness:** You notice triggers and respond to them with curiosity and compassion.
- **Greater Confidence:** You feel more comfortable expressing your true self, including traits you once suppressed.
- **Deeper Relationships:** Your connections feel more authentic and fulfilling.
- **Expanded Creativity:** You approach challenges with fresh perspectives and ideas.

JOURNAL PROMPTS AND WORKSHEET: CHAPTER 7

Reflective Journal Prompts

What shadow traits have I transformed into strengths? How have these traits enriched my life?

_____

_____

_____

_____

Think of a recent situation where I acted with authenticity. What shadow traits did I embrace in that moment?

_____

_____

_____

_____

What limiting beliefs have I reframed through shadow work? How have these new beliefs influenced my actions?

_____

_____

_____

_____

What relationships have improved as a result of my shadow work? What changes have I noticed in how I connect with others?

_____

_____

Worksheet: Transforming Shadow Traits into Strengths

Use this worksheet to reflect on how your shadow traits can support your growth.

What shadow trait have I recently identified?

What strengths or qualities does this trait represent?

How can I use this trait constructively in my life?

What actions can I take to integrate this trait into my relationships or goals?

_____
_____
_____
_____

END-OF-CHAPTER EXERCISE

Write a letter to your shadow, celebrating the transformation you've achieved so far. Reflect on the ways it has contributed to your growth and express gratitude for its role in your journey.

Example Letter:

"Dear Shadow,

Thank you for being my teacher and guide. The parts of myself I once hid have become sources of strength and inspiration. I promise to continue honoring you and learning from your wisdom. Together, we are creating a life that is true to who I am."

Write your letter below:

_____
_____
_____
_____
_____
_____
_____
_____
_____
_____

Chapter 8
LIVING IN WHOLENESS

As the shadow becomes integrated into our awareness, a new chapter of life begins—one of wholeness, authenticity, and ongoing growth. Living in wholeness is not about achieving perfection or eliminating challenges; it's about embracing the complexity of being human. By welcoming both light and shadow, we create a balanced and harmonious relationship with ourselves and the world around us.

This chapter explores what it means to live in wholeness, offering practical tips for maintaining balance, nurturing authenticity, and continuing your shadow work journey.

WHAT DOES LIVING IN WHOLENESS MEAN?

Living in wholeness involves accepting every part of yourself, including the traits and emotions you once disowned. It means stepping into your full humanity—messy, complex, and beautiful.

Key aspects of wholeness

- **Self-Acceptance:** Wholeness begins with accepting yourself as you are, without judgment or shame.
- **Balance:** Integration creates balance between your inner and outer worlds, helping you navigate challenges with resilience.
- **Authenticity:** Living in wholeness allows you to express your true self in all areas of life, free from the fear of rejection.

THE ROLE OF SHADOW WORK IN WHOLENESS

Shadow work doesn't end when you feel integrated—it evolves into a lifelong practice of self-awareness and growth. New experiences, relationships, and challenges will continue to reveal layers of your shadow, offering opportunities for deeper understanding.

WHY ONGOING SHADOW WORK MATTERS

It keeps you connected to your inner truth.

It helps you navigate life's transitions with grace and insight.

It ensures that you continue to grow and adapt as a person.

CULTIVATING A LIFE OF WHOLENESS

To live in wholeness, you must actively nurture the practices, relationships, and mindsets that support your authenticity.

PRACTICE RADICAL SELF-ACCEPTANCE.

Self-acceptance is the foundation of wholeness. It means embracing both your strengths and imperfections with compassion.

Practicing self-acceptance:

- **Acknowledge Your Humanity:** Remind yourself that no one is perfect and that growth is a journey, not a destination.
- **Challenge Self-criticism:** Replace harsh inner dialogue with kind and supportive self-talk.
- **Celebrate Your Growth:** Reflect on the progress you've made and honor your efforts, no matter how small.

Example:

Sarah, a teacher, often felt guilty for needing rest. Through shadow work, she realized this guilt stemmed from childhood messages that equated rest with laziness. By practicing self-acceptance, Sarah reframed rest as an act of self-care, allowing her to recharge without judgment.

Build authentic relationships.

Wholeness thrives in connection. Surrounding yourself with people who honor your authentic self creates a supportive environment for continued growth.

TIPS FOR AUTHENTIC CONNECTION:

- **Share Your Journey:** Openly discuss your shadow work insights with trusted loved ones, fostering deeper understanding and intimacy.
- **Set Boundaries:** Protect your energy by establishing boundaries with those who don't respect your growth.
- **Seek Like-Minded Communities:** Join groups or workshops focused on personal development where you can share and learn from others.

EMBRACE ONGOING GROWTH

Living in wholeness means staying open to new lessons and challenges. Treat each experience as an opportunity to deepen your understanding of yourself and the world.

HOW TO EMBRACE GROWTH

- **Stay Curious:** Approach new experiences with curiosity rather than fear.
- **Revisit Your Shadow:** Periodically reflect on triggers, patterns, or traits that arise in new situations.
- **Expand Your Horizons:** Explore new practices, ideas, or creative outlets that align with your evolving self.

Example:

Mark, a retiree, found himself feeling restless after years of structured work life. Shadow work revealed a suppressed desire for adventure. By pursuing hobbies like travel and photography, Mark embraced this new chapter with excitement and purpose.

NAVIGATING CHALLENGES IN WHOLENESS

Living in wholeness doesn't mean life will always be easy. Challenges and setbacks will still arise, but your shadow work practice equips you to navigate them with greater awareness and resilience.

COMMON CHALLENGES AND SOLUTIONS

Falling Back into Old Patterns: Stress or external pressures may lead you to revert to familiar behaviors.

Solution: Reflect on the situation with compassion. Ask, "What is this teaching me about myself?"

Fear of Vulnerability: Sharing your authentic self can feel intimidating, especially in new relationships or environments.

Solution: Take small steps to build trust, reminding yourself that vulnerability is a strength.

Judgment from Others: Not everyone will understand or support your growth.

Solution: Focus on your own values and priorities. Surround yourself with people who celebrate your authenticity.

PERSONAL REFLECTIONS: STORIES OF LIVING IN WHOLENESS

Elise's Story: Honoring Her Emotions

Elise, a therapist, spent years suppressing her own emotions while helping others navigate theirs. Shadow work taught her to honor her feelings as valid and necessary. By living in wholeness, Elise found greater fulfillment in both her personal and professional life.

Tom's Story: Balancing Strength and Sensitivity

Tom, a firefighter, long believed that showing emotions was a sign of weakness. Shadow work helped him see vulnerability as a complement to his strength. By embracing his emotional side, Tom deepened his relationships and became a more empathetic leader in his community.

THE RIPPLE EFFECT OF WHOLENESS

When we live in wholeness, our transformation extends beyond ourselves. By embracing our shadow, we inspire others to do the same. This ripple effect creates a more compassionate and connected world.

WAYS TO SHARE YOUR WHOLENESS:

Be a role model for authenticity in your relationships.

Share your shadow work journey with others to encourage self-discovery.

Use your strengths to contribute positively to your community.

JOURNAL PROMPTS AND WORKSHEET: CHAPTER 8

Reflective Journal Prompts

What does living in wholeness mean to me? How can I embody this in my daily life?

_____

_____

_____

_____

What self-care practices support my sense of balance and authenticity?

_____

_____

_____

_____

How can I nurture my relationships to reflect and honor my wholeness?

_____

_____

_____

_____

What challenges do I anticipate as I continue this journey? How can I approach them with resilience and compassion?

_____

_____

Worksheet: Creating a Wholeness Plan

Use this worksheet to design a plan for maintaining balance and authenticity in your life.

_____

_____

_____

What daily practices will I use to stay connected to my wholeness?

_____

_____

_____

_____

What relationships or communities will support my ongoing growth?

_____

_____

_____

_____

What values or goals will guide my decisions moving forward?

_____

_____

_____

_____

How will I celebrate and honor my progress along the way?

_____

_____

_____

_____

END-OF-CHAPTER EXERCISE

Write a letter to your future self, reflecting on what living in wholeness means to you. Share your hopes, intentions, and commitment to embracing your full self.

Example Letter:

"Dear Future Me,

I hope you continue to live with courage and authenticity, embracing every part of who you are. Remember that your shadow is a source of strength and wisdom, and that living in wholeness is a journey, not a destination. Celebrate your growth, honor your values, and keep inspiring others by being your true self."

Write your letter below:

_____

_____

_____

_____

_____

_____

_____

_____

_____

_____

Chapter 9
STAYING CONNECTED TO YOUR SHADOW WORK JOURNEY

The process of shadow work doesn't end with integration; it's a lifelong commitment to self-awareness, growth, and authenticity. Staying connected to your shadow work journey means cultivating practices and mindsets that allow you to revisit, reflect on, and deepen your understanding of your shadow as life evolves.

This chapter focuses on building a sustainable shadow work practice, including tips for ongoing reflection, engaging with supportive communities, and adapting your journey to meet new challenges and experiences.

THE LIFELONG NATURE OF SHADOW WORK

Shadow work isn't about "fixing" yourself or reaching a final destination. Instead, it's about developing a dynamic relationship with your shadow—a relationship that grows and evolves as you do.

WHY CONNECTION IS ESSENTIAL

- **New Layers Emerge Over Time:** Each phase of life brings new challenges and opportunities, revealing aspects of the shadow you haven't yet explored.

- **Reinforces Integration:** Regular engagement helps you maintain the balance and authenticity achieved through integration.
- **Prepares You for Change:** Staying connected to your shadow work equips you to navigate transitions and disruptions with resilience and insight.

PRACTICES FOR STAYING CONNECTED

Maintaining a shadow work practice requires consistency and adaptability. These practices can help you stay grounded and connected to your journey.

1. **REGULAR REFLECTION AND JOURNALING**

Journaling is one of the most effective tools for staying connected to your shadow. By reflecting on your thoughts, emotions, and experiences, you can uncover patterns and deepen your understanding.

Prompts for Ongoing Reflection:

"What emotional triggers have I noticed recently? What do they reveal about my shadow?"

"What parts of myself have I been avoiding? Why?"

"How has my shadow influenced my recent decisions or relationships?"

2. **MINDFUL CHECK-INS**

Mindfulness helps you stay present with your emotions and reactions, making recognizing when your shadow is at play easier.

Daily mindfulness practices:

- **Body Scan Meditation:** Tune into physical sensations, noting areas of tension or discomfort.
- **Emotional Awareness:** Pause throughout the day to ask, "What am I feeling right now? What might this emotion be telling me?"

3. EMBRACING LIFE'S TRIGGERS

Triggers are opportunities for growth. By staying curious about your reactions, you can continue to learn from your shadow.

STEPS TO WORK WITH TRIGGERS:

- **Identify the trigger:** What situation or person evoked a strong emotional response?
- **Reflect:** What does this reaction reveal about your hidden fears, desires, or beliefs?
- **Act:** Use this insight to make conscious choices aligned with your values.

4. ENGAGING WITH COMMUNITY

Shadow work can feel isolating, but connecting with others who share similar goals can provide support and inspiration.

WAYS TO BUILD A SUPPORTIVE NETWORK:

Join shadow work groups or personal development workshops.

Participate in online forums or social media communities focused on inner growth.

Share your journey with trusted friends, family, or a therapist.

NAVIGATING CHALLENGES IN STAYING CONNECTED

Even with the best intentions, it's natural to face challenges in maintaining your shadow work practice. Here are some common obstacles and strategies to overcome them:

1. FEELING STUCK

You might feel like you're no longer making progress or that the insights have stopped coming.

Solution: Revisit earlier exercises, journals, or triggers to gain a fresh perspective. Explore new shadow work techniques or revisit unresolved layers.

2. **AVOIDANCE**

Life's busyness or emotional discomfort might lead you to avoid shadow work altogether.

Solution: Start small. Set aside just 5-10 minutes for reflection or mindfulness each day. Remind yourself of the benefits you've experienced from shadow work.

3. **LACK OF SUPPORT**

You may feel unsupported by those around you or struggle to find like-minded individuals.

Solution: Seek out communities, workshops, or online resources. Consider working with a therapist or coach who understands shadow work.

EXPANDING YOUR PRACTICE

As you grow, your shadow work practice should evolve to reflect your changing needs and goals.

1. **EXPLORE ADVANCED TECHNIQUES**

Deepen your practice by experimenting with advanced shadow work methods, such as dream analysis, ancestral healing, or creative expression.

2. **INCORPORATE NEW TOOLS**

Try integrating tools like guided meditations, music or art therapy into your practice to uncover new layers of insight.

3. **REVISIT CORE THEMES**

Reflect on patterns or traits you've already worked with. How have they evolved? What new lessons are they teaching you?

PERSONAL REFLECTIONS: STORIES OF ONGOING SHADOW WORK

Amara's Story: Revising Old Patterns

Amara, a nurse, noticed she was feeling resentful at work, a pattern she had previously addressed in her shadow work. Revisiting her journals revealed that this resentment stemmed from taking on too much responsibility without setting boundaries. By renewing her commitment to self-care, Amara was able to restore balance and let go of the resentment.

Ben's Story: Discovering New Depths

Ben, a musician, had explored his shadow through creative expression. However, after becoming a father, new emotions surfaced, such as fear of failure and inadequacy. By staying connected to his shadow work practice, Ben approached these feelings with curiosity, transforming them into opportunities for personal growth and connection with his child.

SIGNS OF A HEALTHY SHADOW WORK PRACTICE

How can you tell if you're staying connected to your shadow work? Here are some indicators:

- **Increased Self-Awareness:** You notice your emotions, triggers, and patterns with greater clarity.
- **Emotional Flexibility:** You can navigate challenges and setbacks without judgment or avoidance.
- **Deeper Relationships:** You experience more authentic and empathetic connections with others.
- **Continued Growth:** You remain curious and open to learning, even when it feels uncomfortable.

JOURNAL PROMPTS AND WORKSHEET: CHAPTER 9

Reflective Journal Prompts

What practices have helped me stay connected to my shadow work journey? How can I make them sustainable?

_____
_____
_____
_____

What new challenges or experiences are revealing parts of my shadow? How can I approach these with curiosity and compassion?

_____
_____
_____
_____

What support or community do I need to deepen my shadow work practice? How can I seek it out?

_____
_____
_____
_____

How has my shadow work journey transformed my sense of self and relationships?

_____
_____
_____
_____

Worksheet: Building a Sustainable Shadow Work Practice

Use this worksheet to create a plan for staying connected to your shadow work journey.

_____
_____
_____
_____

What practices will I use to stay reflective and mindful?

_____
_____
_____
_____

How will I handle setbacks or moments of resistance?

_____
_____
_____
_____

What new techniques or tools would I like to explore?

_____
_____
_____

Who or what will support me on this journey?

_____
_____
_____

END-OF-CHAPTER EXERCISE

Write a letter to yourself, affirming your commitment to staying connected to your shadow work journey. Reflect on how far you've come and express your dedication to ongoing growth.

Example Letter:

"Dear Self,

I'm proud of the courage and commitment I've shown in my shadow work journey so far. I know this process is not always easy, but I trust in my ability to keep growing and learning. I promise to approach every new challenge with curiosity and compassion, knowing that each step brings me closer to living authentically. I will honor this journey and continue to nurture the relationship I've built with myself."

Write your letter below:

Chapter 10
THE COLLECTIVE SHADOW

UNDERSTANDING OUR SHARED HUMANITY

While shadow work is deeply personal, it is also part of a larger, collective process. The collective shadow refers to the hidden aspects of society—the unconscious beliefs, biases, and fears that shape our collective reality. Just as individuals have their shadows, so too do communities, cultures, and even nations. Understanding the collective shadow allows us to gain insight into how social systems, collective trauma, and shared values shape our behaviors and interactions.

In this final chapter, we will explore the collective shadow, how it manifests in the world around us, and how we can engage with it to foster healing, growth, and unity.

WHAT IS THE COLLECTIVE SHADOW?

The collective shadow consists of the shared, unconscious aspects of humanity that we are unwilling or unable to face. These aspects include cultural biases, prejudices, historical traumas, and the dark side of societal ideologies. The collective shadow can manifest in various ways:

- **Social Injustices:** Racism, sexism, and other forms of discrimination are often rooted in collective shadows that refuse to acknowledge the humanity of others.
- **Cultural narratives:** society's ideas of success, beauty, and morality can reflect hidden fears and biases that shape how we value individuals or groups.
- **National and Global Trauma:** Unaddressed historical events such as wars, colonization, and systemic oppression leave a lingering collective wound that continues to affect future generations.

By acknowledging the collective shadow, we take responsibility for the ways in which these hidden forces shape our lives and the world around us.

HOW THE COLLECTIVE SHADOW MANIFESTS

1. **Projection on a Societal Level**

Just as individuals project their shadow traits onto others, societies do the same. We project undesirable traits—such as greed, anger, or fear—onto marginalized groups, labeling them as "other" or less deserving of empathy and compassion.

Example:

Historically, colonizing nations projected their shadow onto indigenous populations, labeling them as "primitive" and justifying exploitation. These projections continue to affect the relationships between these communities today.

2. **Denial and Avoidance**

The collective shadow is often denied or ignored, especially when it challenges the dominant cultural narrative. Societies may avoid acknowledging their darker history or the ongoing impacts of oppression and injustice.

Example:

Many nations still fail to fully acknowledge the trauma of slavery, colonialism, or genocide. This denial perpetuates cycles of discrimination and violence that affect future generations.

3. **Collective Trauma**

Collective trauma refers to the shared wounds and pain experienced by groups of people. These traumas are passed down through generations and often remain unhealed, influencing the behaviors and attitudes of future generations.

Example:

The trauma of war, displacement, and genocide can manifest in the collective psyche, leading to cycles of violence, fear, and mistrust that affect communities for years.

THE ROLE OF SHADOW WORK IN HEALING THE COLLECTIVE SHADOW

Just as individual shadow work leads to personal growth, engaging with the collective shadow can lead to societal healing. By confronting the darkness in our cultures and communities, we can begin to heal the wounds that divide us and build a more compassionate, inclusive world.

1. **Acknowledging the past**

The first step in healing the collective shadow is acknowledging the painful truths of our history. This involves facing uncomfortable realities, such as acknowledging past injustices, recognizing systemic inequalities, and listening to marginalized voices.

STEPS FOR ACKNOWLEDGING THE COLLECTIVE SHADOW:

- **Educate Yourself:** Learn about the history of oppression, discrimination, and injustice in your community, culture, or nation.
- **Listen to marginalized voices:** amplify the voices of those who have been historically silenced. Listen to their experiences and acknowledge their pain.
- **Confront Denial:** Challenge cultural narratives that deny or justify past injustices. Acknowledge the ways in which denial perpetuates harm.

2. **Embracing compassionate action**

Once we have acknowledged the collective shadow, we can begin to take compassionate action to heal it. Healing the collective shadow requires working together to dismantle systems of oppression, challenge harmful cultural beliefs, and foster empathy and understanding.

WAYS TO ENGAGE WITH THE COLLECTIVE SHADOW:

- **Support social movements:** Participate in movements that address inequality, injustice, and human rights.
- **Foster Dialogue:** Create spaces for open and honest conversations about systemic issues, historical trauma, and cultural healing.
- **Practice Empathy:** Approach others with empathy, recognizing that every individual's actions are influenced by societal conditioning and collective pain.

3. **Creating a new narrative**

Healing the collective shadow involves rewriting cultural narratives that promote division and exclusion. By creating new stories that celebrate diversity, equality, and compassion, we can build a more inclusive society.

STEPS TO CREATE A NEW COLLECTIVE NARRATIVE:

- **Reframe cultural beliefs:** challenge beliefs that perpetuate discrimination, fear, and violence. Replace them with values that emphasize shared humanity, kindness, and inclusion.
- **Celebrate Diversity:** Promote cultural diversity in media, art, education, and community spaces. Celebrate the richness of different traditions, identities, and perspectives.
- **Foster Collective Healing:** Support initiatives that focus on collective trauma healing, such as truth and reconciliation processes or community-based healing practices.

PERSONAL REFLECTIONS: STORIES OF ENGAGING WITH THE COLLECTIVE SHADOW

Javier's Story: Working for Social Justice

Javier, a community organizer, became deeply involved in advocating for marginalized communities after shadow work helped him recognize his own biases and prejudices. "I realized I had been complicit in a system that treated people unfairly, even if I didn't consciously agree with it," he said. By confronting his own biases and learning about the history of racial injustice, Javier became a passionate advocate for social justice and began working to dismantle oppressive systems.

Amina's Story: Embracing Cultural Healing

Amina was a counselor who used shadow work to understand her cultural heritage and the collective trauma that shaped her community's history. By embracing her roots and engaging in cultural healing practices, Amina found a sense of empowerment and connectedness to her ancestors. "I had to learn to honor the pain of my people, but also the strength and resilience that come from that pain," she shared. Through this process, Amina became a facilitator of collective healing within her community.

THE COLLECTIVE SHADOW AND GLOBAL HEALING

As individuals work on integrating their personal shadows, they contribute to the healing of the collective shadow. The more people engage in self-awareness and compassion, the more global healing can take place. The world is interconnected, and our individual journeys of self-understanding ripple outward, affecting the larger collective.

1. **Global Movements and Healing**

Global movements that address climate change, human rights, and systemic inequality are part of the process of healing the collective shadow. By engaging with these movements, we can work together to create a more compassionate world.

2. Unity in Diversity

The collective shadow also reveals the importance of embracing diversity—not just in terms of race or culture but also in perspectives, beliefs, and experiences. Healing happens when we recognize the richness of diversity and work together to build a unified, compassionate world.

JOURNAL PROMPTS AND WORKSHEET: CHAPTER 10

Reflective Journal Prompts

What aspects of the collective shadow have I noticed in my own life or culture? How do they influence my beliefs and actions?

_____
_____
_____
_____

What steps can I take to engage with the collective shadow and contribute to societal healing?

_____
_____
_____
_____

How can I support marginalized voices and perspectives in my community or global efforts?

_____
_____
_____
_____

That new cultural or societal narratives do I want to contribute to in the world?

_____
_____
_____
_____

Worksheet: Engaging with the Collective Shadow

Use this worksheet to reflect on your role in engaging with the collective shadow.

_____
_____
_____
_____

What historical or cultural wounds do I feel connected to?

_____
_____
_____
_____

What biases or prejudices have I been conditioned to accept? How can I challenge these in myself?

_____
_____
_____
_____

What actions can I take to promote collective healing in my community or the world?

_____
_____
_____
_____

How can I create or contribute to a new, inclusive cultural narrative?

_____
_____
_____
_____

END-OF-CHAPTER EXERCISE

Write a letter to your community or the world, expressing your commitment to engaging with the collective shadow. Reflect on how you can contribute to global healing and unity.

Example Letter:

"Dear World, I acknowledge the wounds we carry as a collective, and I commit to being part of the healing process. I will engage in conscious reflection, confront my own biases, and work toward creating a more compassionate and inclusive world. Together, we can heal and transform. Let us embrace each other in our shared humanity."

Write your letter below:

Chapter 11
THE POWER OF INTEGRATION IN EVERYDAY LIFE

Integrating the shadow is not just a psychological exercise—it's a way of living. Once we have embraced our shadow and worked with its wisdom, the true test comes when we bring that integration into our everyday lives. Living authentically means using what we have learned through shadow work to navigate daily interactions, decisions, and challenges with more awareness, compassion, and grace.

This chapter explores how to apply shadow work in your day-to-day existence, making it a transformative practice that shapes your reality. We will discuss how to integrate shadow work into your relationships, career, and personal growth, and how this integration leads to a more harmonious, aligned life.

Living authentically means showing up as the full, integrated version of yourself—acknowledging both the light and shadow within you. It requires letting go of the need for approval, perfection, or validation from external sources. Instead, it's about aligning your actions with your core values, embracing both your strengths and imperfections, and stepping into your power as a whole person.

THE ESSENCE OF AUTHENTICITY

- **Self-Expression**: You can freely express your thoughts, emotions, and desires without fear of rejection or judgment.
- **Self-Trust:** You trust yourself to make decisions that align with your true values, even if they are difficult or unpopular.
- **Self-Love:** You embrace and honor all aspects of yourself, both the parts you love and the parts you have struggled with.

Example:

After years of shadow work, Clara, a teacher, started to express her authentic self more in her classroom. She no longer suppressed her playful side, allowing her creativity and joy to shine through. This shift made her more connected to her students and brought a renewed sense of passion to her work.

SHADOW WORK IN RELATIONSHIPS

One of the most profound areas where shadow work shows its impact is in our relationships. Whether with family, friends, or romantic partners, the way we interact with others is often influenced by our unconscious projections, unresolved emotional wounds, and suppressed traits. By consciously applying shadow work principles, we can transform the way we connect with others and create deeper, more meaningful relationships.

1. REDUCING PROJECTIONS

Projection occurs when we attribute qualities we deny in ourselves to others. For example, if we judge someone as arrogant, it may be because we suppress our own confidence or assertiveness. Shadow work helps us recognize these projections and take responsibility for our own emotions and behaviors.

STEPS FOR REDUCING PROJECTIONS IN RELATIONSHIPS:

- **Notice your emotional reactions:** if you feel strongly about a characteristic in someone else, ask yourself, "What does this remind me of in myself?"
- **Reclaim the projected trait:** acknowledge the part of yourself that has been suppressed and begin to express it in a healthy way.
- **Communicate with empathy:** When you understand your projections, you can communicate more openly and honestly with others, fostering deeper connection and understanding.

Example:

David, a manager, used to feel frustrated with his employee's assertiveness, often interpreting it as "disrespect." Shadow work helped David realize that his discomfort stemmed from his own suppressed assertiveness. By embracing his own voice and supporting his employee's confidence, David strengthened his leadership and improved team dynamics.

2. SETTING HEALTHY BOUNDARIES

Boundary-setting is an essential part of shadow work. Often, we fail to set boundaries because of fears rooted in our shadow, such as fear of rejection, abandonment, or conflict. By integrating the lessons of shadow work, we can set clear and compassionate boundaries that honor our needs and protect our well-being.

STEPS FOR HEALTHY BOUNDARY SETTING:

- **Identify your needs and limits:** What do you need to feel safe and respected in relationships?
- **Communicate with clarity:** Use "I" statements to express your boundaries, such as "I need some alone time to recharge" or "I am not comfortable with this behavior."
- **Practice consistency:** healthy boundaries require regular reinforcement. Stand firm in your limits, but do so with kindness and respect for others.

Example:

Sophia, a caregiver, often felt overwhelmed by the demands of her family. Shadow work helped her recognize that she was neglecting her own needs to please others. By setting clear boundaries and prioritizing self-care, Sophia restored balance in her relationships and began to feel more supported and fulfilled.

SHADOW WORK IN CAREER AND PURPOSE

Our shadow also influences our professional lives. Unacknowledged fears, insecurities, or desires can hold us back from pursuing our goals, taking risks, or expressing our true purpose. Integrating the shadow can help us align our career choices with our authentic selves, leading to greater fulfillment, creativity, and success.

1. **Overcoming Imposter Syndrome:** Imposter syndrome is a common experience where we doubt our abilities and feel like fraud. It often stems from the shadow—specifically, a lack of self-worth or unresolved fears about failure. By integrating these aspects, we can overcome imposter syndrome and step into our full potential.

STEPS FOR OVERCOMING IMPOSTER SYNDROME:

- **Acknowledge your accomplishments:** Take time to celebrate your achievements and remind yourself of your capabilities.
- **Reframe failure:** View failure as an opportunity for growth, not a reflection of your worth.
- **Affirm your worthiness:** Repeat affirmations that reinforce your value, such as "I am capable, worthy, and deserving of success.

Example:

Terry, a graphic designer, often doubted his abilities, despite years of experience. Through shadow work, he realized his imposter syndrome stemmed from childhood messages about not being "good enough." By embracing his talents and achievements, Terry gained the confidence to seek higher-profile clients and expand his career.

2. **Aligning with Your Purpose:** Shadow work can also help you discover and align with your true purpose. As we uncover suppressed desires and passions, we can make conscious choices that bring us closer to our authentic calling.

STEPS TO ALIGN WITH YOUR PURPOSE:

Aligned action: set clear goals and take practical steps that align with your authentic self and purpose.

Example:

Emma, a corporate lawyer, had always secretly wanted to become a writer. Shadow work revealed that her fear of judgment and failure had kept her from pursuing this dream. By integrating her passion for writing and taking small steps toward her goal, Emma eventually transitioned to a full-time writing career, experiencing deeper fulfillment and alignment.

PERSONAL REFLECTIONS: STORIES OF SHADOW WORK IN EVERYDAY LIFE

Raul's Story: Reclaiming Joy

Raul, a father and teacher, had always been serious and focused on providing for his family. Through shadow work, he realized that he had suppressed his playful side to meet societal expectations of responsibility. By reclaiming this part of himself, Raul began to enjoy life more fully, engaging in hobbies and activities that brought him joy. This not only enhanced his well-being but also deepened his connection with his children.

Isabelle's Story: Embracing Vulnerability in Leadership

Isabelle, a CEO, had always kept her vulnerability hidden, fearing it would undermine her authority. Shadow work helped her recognize that vulnerability is a strength, not a weakness. By embracing her vulnerability and openly sharing her struggles, Isabelle created a more transparent and supportive workplace, fostering trust and collaboration among her team.

SUSTAINING SHADOW WORK IN EVERYDAY LIFE

Living in alignment with your shadow and authenticity requires ongoing commitment. By cultivating a practice of self-reflection, setting boundaries, and embracing vulnerability, you can continue to grow and integrate new aspects of yourself as life unfolds.

1. **DAILY INTEGRATION PRACTICES**

- **Mindfulness:** Stay present with your emotions and reactions throughout the day.
- **Journaling:** Use journaling to reflect on your experiences and how your shadow is showing up in everyday life.
- **Affirmations:** Repeat affirmations that reinforce your values and help you embrace your shadow traits in healthy ways.

2. **LONG-TERM INTEGRATION STRATEGIES**

- **Check-Ins:** Regularly assess your progress and revisit past shadow work exercises.
- **Creative Expression:** Continue to use creative outlets to express the parts of yourself that are often suppressed.
- **Community Support:** Seek out communities or individuals who support your journey of authenticity and self-discovery.

JOURNAL PROMPTS AND WORKSHEET: CHAPTER 11

Reflective Journal Prompts

What shadow traits have I integrated into my daily life? How have they enhanced my relationships or care for others?

_____

_____

_____

_____

How can I continue to embrace vulnerability and authenticity in my relationships?

_____

_____

_____

_____

What steps can I take today to align my actions with my true purpose?

_____

_____

_____

_____

How has shadow work helped me grow in my career or personal life? What new opportunities or insights have emerged?

_____
_____
_____
_____

Worksheet: Shadow Work in Daily Life

Use this worksheet to design an ongoing integration plan.

_____
_____
_____
_____

What shadow traits do I want to embrace today?

_____
_____
_____
_____

What practices will I use to stay connected to my authentic self?

_____
_____
_____
_____

How will I continue to challenge limiting beliefs and align with my purpose?

_____
_____
_____
_____

END-OF-CHAPTER EXERCISE

Write a letter to your future self, celebrating your progress and reflecting on how shadow work has transformed your everyday life.

Example Letter:

"Dear Future Me, I am proud of the work I've done to embrace my whole self. The journey has been challenging, but I trust in my ability to continue integrating my shadow and living authentically. I celebrate the growth I've made and look forward to the continued transformation ahead."

Write your letter below:

_____
_____
_____
_____
_____
_____
_____
_____
_____

Chapter 12
REFLECTING ON THE JOURNEY

EMBRACING YOUR WHOLE SELF

As we come to the end of this journey, it's essential to pause and reflect on the profound changes that have occurred through your shadow work process. The path to self-awareness, integration, and authenticity is not linear—it's a continuous cycle of discovery, acceptance, and transformation. This chapter encourages you to look back on the work you've done, honor the progress you've made, and appreciate the person you've become along the way.

Here, we'll explore how to reflect on your journey, celebrate your achievements, and continue the process of shadow integration as a lifelong practice.

THE POWER OF REFLECTION

Reflection is a powerful tool in the journey of shadow work. It allows us to see the growth we've made, the challenges we've overcome, and the lessons we've learned. When we take the time to reflect, we can gain clarity, acknowledge our progress, and deepen our commitment to our ongoing journey of self-discovery.

WHY REFLECTION MATTERS

- **Acknowledging Growth:** Reflection allows us to see how far we've come and appreciate the small victories along the way.
- **Learning from Challenges:** offers an opportunity to reflect on setbacks and how we can use them as learning experiences.
- **Deepening Self-Awareness:** By looking back, we can see new aspects of our shadow that may have emerged and further integrate them.

Example:

Mia had been working on integrating her anger, which she had repressed for years. By taking time to reflect on her journey, she realized how far she'd come—from initially fearing her anger to now expressing it constructively in her relationships. This reflection reinforced her confidence in continuing her shadow work practice.

CELEBRATING YOUR PROGRESS

As you reflect on your shadow work journey, it's essential to celebrate the progress you've made, no matter how small it may seem. Each step forward—whether it's a moment of self-awareness, a shift in perspective, or a difficult conversation—is a victory in itself.

HOW TO CELEBRATE YOUR PROGRESS

- **Acknowledge Milestones:** Celebrate the moments when you faced difficult truths, when you let go of limiting beliefs, or when you had breakthroughs in understanding.
- **Honor Small Victories:** Even the smallest change—such as recognizing a projection or setting a boundary—is worth acknowledging.
- **Create Rituals of Celebration:** Light a candle, take a walk, or treat yourself to something special to honor your progress.

Example:

After a period of deep introspection, Robert celebrated his ability to express vulnerability at work. He acknowledged that, for years, he had been afraid to show his emotions, but shadow work had allowed him to embrace this side of himself. He celebrated this newfound strength by taking time to reflect on how it had positively affected his career and relationships.

LOOKING FORWARD: CONTINUING YOUR SHADOW WORK JOURNEY

Shadow work is not a task to complete; it's a journey that will continue to unfold throughout your life. New layers of your shadow will reveal themselves in different phases of your life, and each time you meet these layers with compassion and awareness, you move closer to living fully and authentically.

1. **SHADOW WORK AS A LIFELONG PRACTICE**

The integration of your shadow doesn't end at the completion of this book—it continues as a lifelong practice. As you go through different life stages—whether it's parenthood, career shifts, or personal challenges—new shadows will surface for you to explore. The key is to remain curious, open, and compassionate as these new aspects emerge.

2. **STAYING OPEN TO CHANGE**

As you continue your journey, remember that shadow work is dynamic. Life will offer new experiences, relationships, and challenges, all of which have the potential to bring forward more of your shadow. The more open and accepting you are of change, the more easily you'll navigate these moments with grace.

Example:

Claire had worked through several layers of her shadow, but during a difficult period in her life, she noticed that new feelings of inadequacy and self-doubt were surfacing. Rather than resisting these emotions, she embraced them as opportunities for deeper shadow work, knowing that they were just another part of her personal evolution.

THE GIFTS OF THE SHADOW

As you reflect on your shadow work, it's important to recognize the gifts your shadow has brought you. The shadow contains aspects of yourself that you've repressed, but it also holds immense power, creativity, and wisdom. By integrating the shadow, you are reclaiming these gifts and learning how to express them in healthy and constructive ways.

THE HIDDEN GIFTS OF YOUR SHADOW

Creativity and Passion: Repressed emotions like anger or sadness can fuel creativity and motivation when acknowledged and expressed.

Resilience: The shadow often holds the parts of you that have endured pain and hardship, making you stronger and more resilient.

Authenticity and Compassion: The more you embrace your shadow, the more authentically you can show up in your life, and the more compassion you will feel for others on their own journeys.

Example:

Sophia, who had struggled with perfectionism, found that embracing her shadow led her to a deeper sense of creativity and self-expression. By allowing herself to make mistakes and embrace imperfection, she unlocked new artistic talents and gained greater freedom in her personal and professional life.

ENGAGING WITH THE WORLD FROM WHOLENESS

As you integrate your shadow and embrace your whole self, you are better equipped to engage with the world around you. You can move through life with greater ease, knowing that you are fully aligned with who you are. The more you live from a place of wholeness, the more you inspire others to do the same.

1. **LEADING BY EXAMPLE**

By continuing to integrate your shadow, you become a role model for those around you, showing others the power of self-awareness and compassion. You can create a ripple effect, inspiring those in your circle to embark on their own journeys of self-discovery.

2. **EMBRACING GLOBAL WHOLENESS**

Shadow work doesn't only happen on the individual level—it can also inspire collective healing. As you continue your journey, look for ways to bring the insights from your shadow work into larger social, cultural, or global movements. Share your wisdom with others, and be a part of creating a world that values authenticity, empathy, and connection.

Example:

Maya, after years of shadow work, began using her experiences to teach mindfulness and emotional intelligence to children. By sharing her insights, she not only helped the children in her community but also inspired their parents to engage in their own shadow work, creating a ripple effect of healing and awareness.

JOURNAL PROMPTS AND WORKSHEET: CHAPTER 12

REFLECTIVE JOURNAL PROMPTS

What milestones have I reached on my shadow work journey? What lessons have I learned along the way?

_____

_____

_____

_____

How can I celebrate the progress I've made in shadow work? What rituals or practices will help me honor my growth?

_____

_____

_____

_____

What new layers of my shadow have emerged, and how can I approach them with compassion and curiosity?

_____

_____

_____

_____

What are the gifts I've discovered through integrating my shadow? How can I use these gifts in my life moving forward?

_____

_____

_____

_____

Worksheet: Reflecting on Your Shadow Work Journey

Use this worksheet to reflect on your shadow work journey and plan for the future.

_____

_____

_____

_____

What have been the most significant insights from my shadow work?

_____

_____

_____

_____

How will I continue integrating my shadow into my daily life?

_____

_____

_____

_____

What steps will I take to share my wisdom and experiences with others?

_____
_____
_____
_____

How can I contribute to global healing and create a world of greater wholeness?

_____
_____
_____
_____

END-OF-CHAPTER EXERCISE

Write a letter to your future self, affirming your commitment to continued shadow work and living authentically. Reflect on your journey and express your intentions for the future.

Example Letter:

"Dear Future Me, I am proud of the journey I've taken and the person I've become. As I continue to grow and integrate more aspects of myself, I promise to approach life with compassion, curiosity, and authenticity. I trust in my ability to face whatever challenges arise and to continue evolving into the fullest version of myself."

Write your letter below:

CONCLUSION
A LIFE TRANSFORMED

As you reach the end of this journey, take a moment to pause and reflect. What began as a path of self-exploration has blossomed into a profound transformation. You've walked through the shadows, faced your fears, and embraced the hidden parts of yourself with compassion and curiosity. This journey has been one of growth, discovery, and ultimately, empowerment.

Through shadow work, you have learned to reconnect with your whole self—acknowledging both your light and your darkness. You have peeled back the layers of your unconscious mind, rediscovering strengths, healing old wounds, and reclaiming parts of yourself that you once denied. With each step, you've moved closer to authenticity and a deeper sense of inner peace.

KEY TAKEAWAYS

- **Self-Awareness Leads to Freedom:** By understanding your shadow, you've learned to recognize your unconscious patterns and emotional triggers. This awareness empowers you to make conscious choices and break free from old, limiting beliefs.

- **Integration is a Lifelong Journey:** Shadow work is not about perfection; it's about embracing all parts of who you are. Integration is ongoing—new layers of your shadow will surface as you grow, but each layer you face brings you closer to living your fullest, most authentic life.

- **Healing Through Compassion:** As you have learned, shadow work is rooted in self-compassion. The more you love and accept yourself—imperfections and all—the more you can offer that love to others. Your shadow is not something to fear but a source of wisdom and strength.
- **Transformation is Possible:** The progress you've made is real. You've cultivated resilience, emotional awareness, and a deeper understanding of your true self. With these tools, you are more capable of navigating life's challenges and embracing your personal power.

EMBRACE YOUR JOURNEY AS A SOURCE OF STRENGTH

As you move forward, remember that your journey is far from over. You've only just begun to tap into your true potential. The shadow you once feared is now a trusted ally, guiding you toward greater authenticity and fulfillment.

Each challenge you encounter from here on out is an opportunity for growth. Every emotional trigger, every difficult conversation, and every moment of self-doubt is simply a new doorway leading to deeper self-understanding. Embrace these moments with the same courage and curiosity you've cultivated in this process.

You have transformed. You are stronger, wiser, and more connected to your inner truth. And as you continue this journey, know that you carry with you the strength of your shadow—integrated, honored, and loved.

Thank you for taking this step toward a more authentic and empowered life. You are not just a person who has worked through their shadow; you are someone who now lives with the full spectrum of their humanity, capable of infinite growth and transformation.

CELEBRATE YOUR PROGRESS AND KEEP GOING

As you celebrate this milestone, remember that this work is not a one-time task. Shadow work is a lifelong practice, one that will continue to unfold with each new chapter of your life. The more you live from a place of wholeness, the more you inspire others to do the same.

So, keep walking this path with love and courage. You are not only transforming your own life; you are contributing to the healing and growth of the collective. Your journey is a testament to the power of self-awareness, compassion, and the unwavering strength of the human spirit.

Embrace the entirety of who you are—both light and shadow—and let your brilliance illuminate the path ahead. This is not the end, but the beginning of your journey.

www.ingramcontent.com/pod-product-compliance
Lightning Source LLC
Chambersburg PA
CBHW041146110526
44590CB00027B/4143